REFORGING THE MAN
YOU ARE NOT BROKEN

By:

Justin Butler Sr.

"For every man who thought he was beyond repair."

Reforging the Man: You Are Not Broken

Copyright © 2025 *by Justin Butler Sr.*

All rights reserved. No part of this publication may be reproduced, stored in a retrieval system, or transmitted in any form or by any means—electronic, mechanical, photocopying, recording, or otherwise—without prior written permission of the publisher, except for brief quotations used in reviews or scholarly works.

First Edition

ISBN 979-8-9932220-0-4

Published by Butler Publishing
Deltona, FL
Cover design by Justin Butler Sr.
Printed in the United States of America

Dedication

*For **every man** who thought he was too far gone—*

For those who walked through fire and silence,

for the sons who still wonder if they matter,

for the fathers who fear they've failed—

this is proof you are not broken.

To my sons, my father, and my brothers in Christ.

To the men who lent me their hand, and to God who whispers,
"You are not broken."

Epigraph

"Even the hardest metal remembers the forge. Even the strongest man remembers what it was like to be weak.

But the fire that scarred you is the same fire that proves you are not broken."

As "Iron sharpeneth iron; so a man sharpeneth the countenance   of his friend."
— **Proverbs 27:17** (AKJV)

The forge is open. The fire is yours.

Table of Contents

Prologue: The Fire and the Silence   **p.VIII**

Chapter One: Fire & Silence
The furnace of boyhood—where the first scars and silences forge the man.   **p.9**

Chapter Two: Broken Inheritance
Wounds passed down like heirlooms—learning you're not bound to repeat the cycle.   **p.17**

Chapter Three: Armor & Masks
Survival means armor, laughter, and lies—until the weight is too much to bear.   **p.25**

Chapter Four: Breaking Point
Where the old armor shatters and the truth finally breaks through.   **p.31**

Chapter Five: Whisper & Turning
A quiet voice in the ashes—inviting a new beginning when everything else is spent.   **p.37**

Chapter Six: Reforging Process
The slow, searing work of becoming whole—hammer, anvil, and grace.   **p.43**

The Marks of the Forge
Interlude: When the Forge Speaks Without a Voice   **p.49**

Chapter Seven: Rising as a Son, Brother, and Father
Restored identity—standing as son, walking as brother, leading as father. **p.51**

Chapter Eight: Wounds Become Weapons
Scars no longer shame—they become strength for the next battle.
p.57

Chapter Nine: Walking Unashamed
No more fig leaves—living free, scars and all. **p.61**

Chapter Ten: The Call to Other Men
Testimony becomes trumpet—calling brothers into the forge.
p.65

Chapter Eleven: The Brotherhood Restored
Rising together—where trust replaces rivalry and scars become shield walls. **p.69**

Chapter Twelve: Fathers of Fire
Breaking old cycles—passing down flame, not ashes. **p.73**

Chapter Thirteen: Sons of Flame
A new generation rises—torch in hand, fear left behind. **p.77**

Chapter Fourteen: The Reforged Legacy
A single life, a generational wildfire—legacy that burns on. **p.81**

Chapter Fifteen: The Weapon of Wisdom
Scars sharpened into wisdom—pain becomes an arsenal against the darkness. **p.87**

Chapter Sixteen: The Quiet General
Strength that leads by presence, not volume—commanding with scars, not threats. **p.91**

Chapter Seventeen: The Forge of Brotherhood
Truth forged in the trenches—no man reforged alone. **p.99**

Chapter Eighteen: The Silent March
Strength proven in quiet endurance—brotherhood walking in the dark, unbroken. **p.105**

Chapter Nineteen: The Final Ascent
The last climb—calling every lesson, every scar, into the open.
p.109

Chapter Twenty: The View From the Summit
The vantage point—seeing scars as strength, brotherhood as proof, and fire as witness. **p.113**

Final Chapter: The Commission: You Are the Fire
The charge—rise, lead, witness. Your story is the torch. **p.117**

Closing Meditation: The Blessing
Every scar tells a story. **p.120**

The Quiet General—Action Page
A little workbook preview. Challenge Yourself. **p.125**

Prologue: The Fire and the Silence

Summary:

There's a fire that never dies in a man, even when the world tries to drown it in silence, shame, or failure. That fire is grace—it flickers, rages, hides, but refuses to be extinguished. This book is the testimony of that fire: how it survives the silence, breaks the shame, and turns wounds into weapons.

Before anything else, this is a book for men who know what it is to hurt, to lose, and to hope again.

Throughout these pages you will encounter what I call **Scroll Echoes** *and* **Reflections**. *Take them as the hammer's strike—meant to jolt you out of reading and into forging. They are not mine to answer—they are yours. These words are set to resonate in the hollow places of a man's soul, where silence hides and wounds wait.*

When you reach them, do not skim. Pause. Let the page become a mirror. Wrestle with the questions. Write if you must, pray if you must, bleed if you must—but do not pass them by untouched. For it is here, in the echo, that the reforging begins.

Chapter One
THE FIRE AND THE SILENCE

Born in the Furnace

Every man carries a fire.

Some are born with it blazing.
Some use up a lifetime searching for one spark.
But all of us learn, sooner or later, the world will try to snuff it out.

I didn't inherit warmth.
I inherited flames.

My childhood wasn't a cradle. It was a burning furnace.
And furnaces don't coddle.
They strip away. They reveal. They burn whatever fuel they have.

I was tossed into the flames, not for destruction, but because others didn't face their own.

People are empowered to carry fire—but it is always their choice to use it, never see it, or abuse it.

Knives in the Passageway

I don't remember bedtime stories.
I remember the sharp smell of smoke,
a table rattling from a slammed fist,
a knife flashing in the hand of my uncle over some borrowed cash my mother didn't have.
That was normal.
That was "home."

My parents were just kids themselves—barely old enough to drive, but already carrying enough brokenness to fill a house. So, I grew up in the fallout: part foster baby, part unwanted son, part witness to a storm I never caused.

Silence became my blanket.
You don't cry in the middle of chaos.
You don't speak unless you want to be screamed at.
You hide what hurts, because if you show it, it will be used against you.

But silence is tricky.
At first, it feels like safety.
Then it becomes a tomb.

Rage as Armor

So I made a vow: *Never again.*

If I couldn't be safe, I would be strong.
If I couldn't be loved, I would be respected.
If I couldn't trust, I would outwork, outlift, outlast.

Rage became my armor.
It gave me strength, but it also stole my rest.

You can build a body out of anger—
stack muscle on your shoulders, grip steel until your hands split,
carry twice what other men can lift.

But you can't build peace out of it.
At night, when the laughter fades and the noise dies down, rage leaves you alone with the silence again.

Laughter as a Mask

Not every scar bled red. Some bled laughter.

Humor was my disguise—the quick trick to keep the wolves at bay.
If I could make you laugh, maybe you wouldn't see how close I was to breaking.
Maybe you wouldn't notice the boy hidden under the armor.

I wore the clown mask,
the strongman mask,
and finally the silent mask when nothing was left to say.

Laughter can sooth anger.
It can also hide a wound so deep that nobody bothers to ask.

A well-placed joke could defuse a fight.
It could hide a wound long enough for me to walk away.
It could give me cover when I felt the wolves circling.

But even then, the disguise was thin.
Because when the laugh faded, I was still the boy under the armor.
And masks—any kind—get heavy.
When you take them off, you're still alone in the silence.

Embers That Would Not Die

And yet—
there were sparks.

Moments when the silence cracked.
Moments when something deeper reached through the smoke and said: I see you.

A hand on my shoulder that didn't demand anything in return.
A word I didn't expect: You're not alone.
A pulse in the dark that felt like truth—older, stronger, more real than my pain.

I didn't have the language yet, but I know it now:
the Spirit was whispering through the noise,
reminding me that the fire in me was not a curse.
It was a gift.

No matter how much the world tried to bury it,
the fire would not die.

✗ The Scroll Echo

Later in life, I would come to understand what that rhythm was—
the pattern that ran under every fight, every silence, every breakthrough.

Ground | Pulse | Swing

> **Ground:** the moments where I stood in the ashes of what broke me.
> **Pulse:** the heartbeat of rage, of laughter, of Spirit, pushing me forward.
> **Swing:** the movement that carried me out of one silence and into another flame.

That rhythm was always there,
hidden under the noise of knives and slammed doors,
carrying me forward even when I thought I was standing still.

What the Fire and the Silence Teach

Here's what I know now:

- **The fire that tried to destroy you was meant to make you whole.**
- **The silence that haunts you was never abandonment—it was the anvil where your soul was being shaped.**

Every scar carries a reverent silence.
And every silence hides a lesson.

You are not positioned with lack.
You are the blade being renewed.

They told me real men don't cry—that pain doesn't matter.
They told me to swallow my anger or encounter more wrath.
They told me to keep family secrets buried, because if no one knows we can pretend and move on.

But the truth is this:
The fire you have was never meant to be hidden.
The silence around you was never meant to wound.
It was meant to give you peace enough to hear truth.

A Word for the Reader

If you're sitting in your own silence right now—
jaw clenched, chest tight, wondering if that fire in you is gone—
hear me: it isn't.

The silence is not the end.
It's the forge.

The fire is not gone.
It's waiting for your breath to flow through it again.

Brother, you are not broken.
You are being reforged.

And the forge is proof that you were always worth the fire.

 **SIDEBAR: For Reflection**

> "Even the hardest metal remembers the forge. Even the strongest man remembers what it was like to be weak."

Answer and forge ahead:

- Where did silence bury me?
- Where did fire keep me alive?
- Which scars are still teaching me today?
- What step can I take today to let silence become strength instead of a tomb?

The Flame Whispers
You did not choose your father's fire.
But you do choose what burns in you.
The chain ends here. The blaze begins again.

Chapter Two
BROKEN INHERITANCE

Born Into Someone Else's Battle

We don't choose the soil we grow in.
We don't pick the family tree.
We don't get to vote on the wounds that run through our blood.

I was born carrying baggage I didn't pack.
Fear, silence, rage—passed down like heirlooms.

Before I ever made a mistake,
before I ever raised my own fist,
I was already standing in the fallout of choices made long before me.

That's what it means to inherit brokenness:
You wake up one day and realize you've been fighting a battle your parents never won.

My Mother's Side

My mother grew up in a house that knew chaos like an old friend.

Abandonment was the story.
Abuse was the language.
Addiction became the rhythm.

She was called her father's favorite, a daughter of six kids—
which only meant she carried the heaviest load.
When her father walked out,
she became the caretaker, the mother to her siblings,

a child forced to act like an adult before she even knew who she was.

Favor came at a cost:
jealousy, violence, betrayal.
She bore scars she never asked for,
and by the time she had me, she was already a survivor, stitched by pain.

But even in that house, faith flickered.
She was confirmed in the church, baptized into a faith that promised hope—
yet the weight she carried made it hard to see that freedom.
Maybe that's why, later, she chose not to talk about her faith with me.
What had been forced in pain, twisted by anger, she refused to repeat.

Brokenness doesn't stay put.
It leaks.
It spills onto the next generation.

My Father's Side

My father's house was full of faith—
but faith without tenderness can turn rigid, hard-edged.

He was one of twelve.
A strict WWII veteran ruled that house, torn by war and skewed by death.
Food was rationed, for lack, cabinets locked,
love measured out like punishment.

They all heard the same scriptures,
but each carried them differently.
Some clung to the words.

Some repeated them but lived them out their way.
Some twisted them into rules that cut more than they healed.

Maybe it was the echoes of their own wounds.
Maybe it was the shadow of the abuse they never spoke about.
Whatever the reason, faith in that house didn't always sound like love.

When my father was a child, an accident changed everything,
For a time, his mother coddled him, as fearful mothers do.
That coddling turned to passivity.
By the time he was grown,
he had skill with his hands but little strength in his heart.

He could fix an engine,
but not a marriage.
He could lift a transmission,
but not a wounded child.

His silence wasn't cruelty.
But absence can feel just as cruel.
And absence wounds as deeply as abuse.

Conception in the Crossfire

They were fifteen.
Fifteen.

Too young to heal themselves,
too broken to build a home,
and yet here I came—
born into the crossfire of two bloodlines,
the child of survival and silence,
destined to carry both burdens until I chose otherwise.

I was fostered out.
Raised by strangers.
Returned to chaos like a lamb to the slaughter.

That's what broken inheritance looks like:
a cycle you didn't start,
a curse you didn't deserve,
but one you're forced to confront if you ever want to walk free.

Rage as Legacy

I used to think my anger was mine alone.
But trace the line—
rage, addiction, silence on both sides.
Pain tempered by violence,
submission disguised as peace.

These forged me:
a man who could lift almost anything
but could not put down his own pain.

Every family passes something down.
Land. Wealth.
Mine passed down wounds.

That's the broken inheritance.

The Crossroads

Here's the truth every man must face:

We inherit what we didn't choose.
But we decide what passes on.

Fire. Silence. Choice.

Will I repeat the cycle,
or will I break it?

✕ The Scroll Echo

Ground | Pulse | Swing

> **Ground:** I stood in the soil of broken ground, roots twisted, poisoned.
> **Pulse:** I felt the heartbeat of rage, silence, laughter, Spirit—pushing me forward anyway.
> **Swing:** I moved—not perfectly, not cleanly, but I moved—out of the inheritance that tried to own me.

A Word for the Reader

Brother, you didn't choose your family's fire.
You didn't pick their silence.
But you are carrying their weight whether you realize it or not.

The question is not whether you inherited brokenness.
The question is: What will you do with it?

Let the silence bury you,
or let the fire refine you.

You are not broken.
You are the point where the cycle ends.

⚒ SIDEBAR: Broken Inheritance

> **"You didn't choose it.
> But you decide what passes on."**

Answer and forge ahead:

- What did I inherit that I never asked for?
- Where do I see rage, silence, or absence repeating in me?
- What do I refuse to hand to the next generation?
- What choice will I make now so my children inherit fire, not silence?

The Flame Whispers
Brother, the silence will not save you.
The cycle will not own you.
Step forward—the fire is waiting.

Chapter Three
ARMOR AND MASKS

The Weight of Survival

By the time I stepped into manhood,
I had already learned two things:

Nobody is coming to save you.

You'd better build something strong enough to carry the weight yourself.

So I did what broken men do—
I built armor.
I put on masks.
I learned to survive.

It worked.
Until it didn't.

Armor Made of Rage

Rage was my first shield.

When the silence cut too deep,
when the wounds throbbed louder than words could cover,
anger came roaring in like a warhorse.

I wore it like steel on my chest.
If they feared me, no one could touch me.
If I struck first, they couldn't hurt me.

In the shop, I lifted castings other men wouldn't touch.
On the floor, I muscled through jobs without the hoist.
At home, I carried burdens nobody asked me to—

because life is expensive, and time is money.

Rage can fuel you.
But it will also consume you.
Rage damages fast.
And nothing grows in its wake.

Humor as a Mask

Remember, laughter was a disguise.

Humor kept wolves off balance.
I made you laugh,
hoping you wouldn't see how I felt inside.

I sought out the clown in every room,
and the strongman in another.
I cracked jokes to hide tears.
I gained smiles while sadness filled my heart.

Humor disarms a rooms tension—
but keeps anyone from asking questions.
It buries pain so deep you forget you even carry it.

Silence as a Prison

Then there was silence.

That old inheritance.
This mask looked the most natural on me.

Silence was easier than explaining.
Easier than being misunderstood again.
I didn't care to listen,
and it had nothing to say.

But silence is not true armor.
It's a prison cell.
And I wore the key around my own neck,
never realizing I could use it to walk free.

The Cracks in the Armor

Here's what I discovered:
Armor keeps people out.
But it also keeps healing out.

The masks may fool others.
But when you're alone, they fool no one.

My rage leaked into the wrong places—
words I never should have spoken to my sons.
My humor sounded hollow, even to my own ears.
My silence left me more alone than safe.

The armor was supposed to protect me.
Instead, it began to crush me.

⚒ The Scroll Echo

Ground | Pulse | Swing

> **Ground:** I stood armored, masked, carrying strength I thought was mine alone.
> **Pulse:** The cracks came—anger spilling, silence choking, laughter failing.
> **Swing:** Spirit whispered: This is not who you are. This is what you built to survive. Lay it down.
> **Lay it down.**
> You were made for more than survival.

The forge of manhood is not about wearing armor.
It's about learning when to take it off.

What Armor Costs

Every man wears armor.
Every man wears masks.
The problem isn't wearing them.
It's forgetting who you are underneath.

Rage may protect you, but it robs you of gentleness.
Humor may cover you, but it can steal your authenticity.
Silence may shield you, but it will strangle your voice.

The very things that save you in battle
can kill you in peace.

A Word for the Reader

Brother, what armor are you wearing today?
What mask have you convinced yourself is "you"?

>Look close:

- Does your anger protect—or isolate?
- Does your humor connect—or deflect?
- Does your silence calm—or imprison?

You are not your armor.
You are not your mask.

Take them off, even if your hands shake.
The man underneath is still alive.
The fire is still there.

⚔ SIDEBAR: Armor and Masks

"The very things that save you in battle can kill you in peace."

Answer and forge ahead:

- What armor did I build to survive my past?
- Where is that armor now holding me back?
- Who am I beneath the mask?
- What mask will I take off this week, even if my hands shake?

The Flame Whispers
Lay it down.
You were never forged to hide.
You were forged to stand in the open, fire in your chest, unashamed.

Chapter Four
THE BREAKING POINT

When the Armor Fails

Every man believes his armor will hold.
That if he straps it tight enough, if he laughs loud enough, if he stays silent long enough—
the cracks will never show.

But armor always fails.
Masks always slip.
And silence always gives way.

For me, the breaking point wasn't dramatic at first.
It was ordinary.
It came in the middle of life,
in the grind of being husband, father, worker, provider.
It came the way storms come—
slow clouds gathering until suddenly the sky splits open.

Rage at the Wrong People

The fire inside me boiled over.
Not on the men who deserved it.
Not on the system that twisted me.
But on the people I loved.

One day, I lashed out at my son.
The words left my mouth before I could catch them.
His eyes—shocked, wounded—
hit me harder than any fist ever had.

In that moment,
I saw it—the fire I thought was armor was a torch in my own hand,

burning down the house I swore to protect.

Rage had turned from armor into a weapon.
And I was the one swinging it against my own blood.

The Weight of Silence

When rage fades, silence moves in.
But silence doesn't heal—it suffocates.

I'd lie awake, jaw tight,
body strong but soul exhausted,
knowing something was breaking inside me.

The silence whispered:
"You're not enough. You'll never change. This is who you are."

That's when I understood—
silence can be louder than shouting.
It can bury a man alive.

At the fracture, when the armor cracks,
it is not your weakness on display.
It is your soul crying for air.

The Mirror Moment

There comes a moment when you catch your own reflection
and can't look away.
I saw the man I'd become.
Strong on the outside, hollow on the inside.
A provider, but not present.
A father, but not patient.
A man, but not whole.

That's the collapse:
When you can't lie to yourself anymore.
When the masks fall,
when the armor shatters,
when you stand naked in your own failure.

And yet—
that's also the doorway.

The Whisper in the Fire

It wasn't thunder that met me.
It wasn't condemnation.
It was a whisper:
"You are not broken. You are being reforged."

For the first time, I saw it—the breaking point was not
condemnation, but goodness and mercy.
It was more than breaking. It was when the forging began.
The place where the hammer falls, not to destroy,
but to shape.

The fire wasn't an enemy I'd need to fight, but a refiner to be
embraced even when guarded and by it.

✖ The Scroll Echo

Ground | Pulse | Swing

> **Ground:** I fell—armor gave way, mask torn, silence deafening.
> **Pulse:** Spirit's whisper broke through: Not broken. Forged.
> **Swing:** I rose—not perfect, not fixed, but willing to be remade.

A Word for the Reader

Brother, if you're standing at the breaking point right now, know this:

It is not the end.
It is the place where the refiner's fire does its work.

The breaking point is not where you die.
It's where the false man dies.
The real man—the reforged man—emerges.

Don't run from the breaking point.
Lean into it—be real with yourself, not hidden.
It may be the first ground that will not lie to you.

⚔ SIDEBAR: When the Armor Gives Way

> **"The breaking point is not where you die.
> It's where the false man dies."**

Answer and forge ahead:

- Where have I seen my armor fail?
- Who have I wounded with the fire meant to protect me?
- What honest conversation will I have because my armor has cracked?
- What would it look like to see my breaking point not as an ending, but as a forge?

The Flame Whispers
The breaking point isn't punishment.
It's permission—
permission to stop pretending,
permission to start becoming.

Chapter Five
THE WHISPER AND THE TURNING

When Noise Finally Fades

The fire had raged.
The armor had cracked.
The silence had nearly suffocated me.

But in the middle of the wreckage,
something else began breaking through.
Not roaring.
Not lecturing.
Not men pretending to know me.

This small whisper, the faintest sound.

The Unexpected Voice

I can't tell you it came through thunder or lightning.
It wasn't bold, written in the sky.

It was quieter—
I should have missed it, if I had not been listening,
for something besides my own humiliation.

I heard it say:
"You are not broken. You are being reforged."

Those words didn't repeat in my ears.
They split through the silence keeping me prisoner in decades.
They shot past me; I wasn't ready to believe them.

A Turning of the Heart

Every man who reaches a breaking point has choices:

Turn back into an old fire, old armor and silence.

Or turn toward something, uncertain and unfamiliar, but alive.

For me, the choice wasn't dramatic.
It was very small.
It was choosing to sit in the quiet and not run.
It was daring to believe what whispered was true.
It was lowering my fist to be present for the first time in years.

That's what turning looks like at the start.
Not fireworks.
Not perfection.
Just one decision: I won't run from this voice.

The First Signs of Life

I started noticing things I acknowledged but ignored:

My son's laughter—the kind I used to have, mine drown out by noise.

My wife's patience—even after all the storms I'd brought through the door.

My own breath—slower, steadier, the anxiety I wasn't choking anymore.

These weren't grand revelations.
They were small mercies.
But small mercies, they are how turning begins.

⚒ The Scroll Echo

Ground | Pulse | Swing

> **Ground:** Silence stripped me down, shame tried to bury me.
> **Pulse:** A whisper cut through: Not broken. Forged.
> **Swing:** I turned—not everything at once, one breath, one step, one choice at a time.

Why the Whisper Mattered

Men are trained to respond to commands,
to shouts,
to challenges.

But the whisper isn't like that.
It doesn't dominate.
It invites. It presses softly.

It doesn't demand proof of yourself.
It reminds you who you already are.

The turning doesn't happen in force.
It happens because you finally believe the whisper more than the lies.

A Word for the Reader

Brother, if you hear anything at all—
that heart whisper in the silence,
a word that doesn't sound like you, and shame,
a reminder that you are more than your scars—

Don't ignore it.
That whisper is grace calling you, and your turning has already begun.

It doesn't matter how small it feels.
Every fire starts small.
Every revolution begins with a single turn.

 SIDEBAR: The Whisper

"You are not broken. You are being reforged."

Answer and forge ahead:

- What small mercies have I overlooked because I expected something louder?
- Where is the whisper cutting through my silence right now?
- What small mercy can I name out loud today as proof I am turning?
- Am I willing to believe—just for today—that I am not broken?

The Flame Whispers
Grace doesn't shout.
It whispers,
and every whisper strong enough
to turn a man back to life.

Chapter Six
THE REFORGING PROCESS

From Shattered to Shaped

The breaking point left me raw.
The whisper left me turning.

But turning is not the same as being whole.
Every blade has to be reforged—
not just picked up off the ground and wiped clean.

A broken sword can't be trusted in battle.
It must be melted, reshaped,
and tempered until the steel sings again.

So it was with me.

The Furnace of Daily Life

Reforging didn't happen in a monastery.
It happened in my garage.
In the break room.
On the living room couch with my kids.

Everyday life became the furnace.

A moment of anger—I had to choose gentleness.
A moment of despair—I had to choose hope.
A moment of silence—I had to choose voice.

Not all at once.
Not perfectly.
But each choice was another hammer strike on the steel of my soul.

Hammer and Anvil

Reforging hurts—I want to scream this—because it meant
facing lies I had carried too long.

There's no way around it.
The hammer falls.
The anvil holds you in place.

Sometimes the hammer is a word from my wife—truth I didn't
want to hear.
Sometimes it's the disappointment in my son's eyes.
Sometimes it's my own reflection,
reminding me I can't go back to who I was.

Each blow stung.
But each one shaped me.

Without the hammer, the steel stays weak.
Without the anvil, it never takes form.

Quenched and Tempered

Once the steel is shaped,
it must be quenched.

Plunged into water,
shocked by the sudden chill.

For me, the quenching came in moments of surrender:
letting go of control,
admitting I couldn't fix myself,
allowing Spirit to do the work I couldn't.

Then came tempering—
the slow reheating,

the measured testing,
the seasons of patience that kept me from shattering again.

Strength is not just about hardness.
It's about resilience.
The blade that refuses to bend will break.
The blade that is tempered can flex and still endure.

⚒ The Scroll Echo

Ground | Pulse | Swing

> **Ground:** Broken steel, lying in the dust.
> **Pulse:** Hammer and anvil shaping, quenching, tempering.
> **Swing:** A weapon reborn—not for destruction, but for defense, healing, and truth.

The Marks of the Forge

Here's the truth:
A reforged blade still bears scars.
The lines where it cracked.
The welds where it was mended.

But those marks are not weakness.
They are proof.

Proof that the steel has been through fire and lived.
Proof that the man has been tested and remains.

The reforged man doesn't hide his scars.
He wields them.
He lets them speak.
He knows his strength doesn't come from pretending to be perfect,

but from surviving the fire and coming out whole.

A Word for the Reader

Brother, if you feel the hammer falling right now,
if you feel pressed against the anvil,
if you feel quenched by shock or tempered by waiting—
don't despise it.

This is the reforging process.
The marks left on you will not make you weak.
They will make you unbreakable.

You are not broken.
You are being reforged.

 **SIDEBAR: The Forge**

> **"Strength is not just about hardness.
> It's about resilience."**

Answer and forge ahead:

- Where is the hammer falling in my life right now?
- What am I resisting that could actually shape me?
- Where can I choose one different response today—gentleness for anger, voice for silence?
- Do I see my scars as proof of weakness—or proof of survival?

The Flame Whispers
Your scars are not shame.
They are proof of the fire—
and the fire has not destroyed you.
It has made you whole.

The Marks of the Forge

Interlude: When the Forge Speaks Without a Voice

I had no mentor.

No hand to guide the hammer.
No father-voice steadying the steel.

Every truth I carry was fought for, bone by bone, scar by scar.
And maybe that's why the marks run so deep.

But these scars are not shame.
They are proof.

Proof I survived the forge alone.
Proof that no man is beyond being reforged.

I said I had no mentor—and it's true in one sense. No father-voice, no steady hand. The people I turned to were absent, selfish, or blind.

But looking back, I see it now: God was there. Not written in the sky. Not knocking at my door. Not through perfect people with pure motives.

He was there in the whispers.
In the so-called coincidences.
In the strength I didn't know I had.

No one came to save me—He had already come.
The unseen Speaker of the forge was there all along.

And every scar I carry is proof of that Presence.
Proof that He reforges men even in silence, even in loneliness, even when everyone else fails.

Oh, and I have stories—tales so deep they will bring disbelief to those who won't hear.

And the fire didn't stop there. It kept working—in places I didn't expect, in choices that tested whether the reforging was real.

Chapter Seven
RISING AS A SON, BROTHER, AND FATHER

The Fruit of the Forge

A reforged blade doesn't stay on the blacksmith's bench.
It's meant to be wielded.

The same is true of the man.
The fire, the hammer, the anvil—they weren't just about me.
They were shaping me for the people I was born to walk beside:
as a son, as a brother, as a father.

Rising as a Son

Before I could be anything else, I had to learn again how to be a son.

Not just a son of my earthly father—
whose silence and passivity left gaps I once cursed.
But a son of the Father who whispered in the fire:
"You are not broken."

To rise as a son meant releasing the bitterness I carried,
even toward men who failed me.
It meant receiving an identity I couldn't earn:
beloved, claimed, called.

A true son doesn't walk in shame.
He walks in the confidence that he belongs.

Rising as a Brother

Brotherhood had always been complicated for me.

I knew rivalry.
I knew betrayal.
I knew how men could compete, cut, and leave each other bleeding.

But rising as a brother meant something different.

- Choosing solidarity over suspicion.
- Standing shoulder-to-shoulder, not face-to-face.
- Protecting the vulnerable instead of preying on them.

Brotherhood is the forge extended outward.
One blade sharpened by another.
Not to wound, but to prepare for battle.

Rising as a Father

The hardest rise was as a father.
Because fatherhood exposes everything you tried to hide.

My son didn't need a man who was always strong.
He needed a man who was always present.
A man who could say "I was wrong."
A man who could admit his fire once burned the wrong way.

Fatherhood isn't about control.
It's about guidance.
It's not about being flawless.
It's about being faithful.

To rise as a father, I had to lay down the mask of perfection.
I had to pick up the mantle of example.

Not 'do as I say.'
But 'walk with me, and see how even broken men can be remade.'

⚒ The Scroll Echo

Ground | Pulse | Swing

Ground: Son—receiving identity.
Pulse: Brother—walking in solidarity.
Swing: Father—leading with presence, not perfection.

The Restoration of Roles

This was the true fruit of the reforging:
not a man who stood alone in the ashes,
but a man who could rise in his rightful place.

Every role restored was a declaration:

- I am not abandoned.
- I am not alone.
- I am not disqualified.

Sonship healed my past.
Brotherhood healed my present.
Fatherhood healed my future.

A Word for the Reader

Brother, wherever you stand—
whether you carry wounds from your father,
loneliness among brothers,
or fear of failing your children—
hear this:

You were made to rise.
Not as a flawless man,
but as a reforged man.

Your roles are not lost.
They are waiting.
And the forge has already prepared you to carry them.

⚔ SIDEBAR: The Three Rises

—Sonship restores identity.
    —Brotherhood restores solidarity.
        —Fatherhood restores legacy.

Answer and forge ahead:

- Which role do I resist stepping into?
- Where has bitterness, rivalry, or shame kept me from rising?
- What would it mean to live as a son, a brother, and a father today?
- What one act will show my sonship, brotherhood, or fatherhood today?

> ***The Flame Whispers***
> *Your roles are not lost.*
> *They were waiting for you all along.*
> *The fire did not take them away—*
> *it prepared you to carry them.*

Chapter Eight
WOUNDS BECOME WEAPONS

Scars That Speak

For years I hid my scars.
I thought they made me weak,
marked me as less than other men.

But the forge taught me something different:
Scars don't signal failure.
They signal survival.

Every wound every silence, every fire—none were wasted.
They were forged into something sharp.

The Turning of Shame

Shame says: "You're broken. Stay quiet."
The whisper said: "You're reforged. Speak."

When I stopped hiding my wounds,
they started healing others.

- The story of my anger gave my son permission to tell me his fears.
- The story of betrayal gave another man courage to trust again.
- The story of silence gave my wife the gift of finally being heard.

My wounds didn't disqualify me.
They became the very tools I needed for the fight.

A Weapon Is Not for Show

A weapon isn't meant to be hung on the wall and admired.
It's meant to be wielded.

The same is true of our scars.
They aren't for self-display.
They're for battle—
for cutting through lies,
for defending the vulnerable,
for showing other men the way out.

A scar doesn't just say, "I was hurt."
It says, "I healed—and you can too."

⚒ The Scroll Echo

Ground | Pulse | Swing

> **Ground:** Wounds once hidden in shame.
> **Pulse:** Scars revealed, turned into testimony.
> **Swing:** Weapons of wisdom, wielded to defend, guide, and heal.

Weapons of Wisdom

Every man carries a different weapon forged from his past:

- The fatherless man carries a blade of compassion for sons.
- The betrayed man carries a shield of discernment against falsehood.
- The addict carries a spear of testimony that pierces despair.
- The angry man carries a hammer of patience that builds instead of breaks.

These aren't trophies.
They're armaments.
And when wielded with mercy,
they turn battles that once destroyed us into victories for others.

The Enemy Trembles

The enemy knows this truth:
A healed man is dangerous.

Because the very tools once used against him
become weapons in his hands.

Chains become whips.
Scars become maps.
Loss becomes fire.

The enemy trembles not at perfect men,
but at reforged men—
because nothing he did was wasted.

A Word for the Reader

Brother, what wounds have you hidden?
What scars do you still treat as shame?

Lay them on the forge.
Let them be reforged into weapons.

Because someone else's freedom
is waiting on your story.

⚔ SIDEBAR: The Scar as Sword

> **"Your greatest wound can become your sharpest weapon."**

Answer and forge ahead:

- What wound have I been too ashamed to reveal?
- What's one way I can share my story this week—openly, not hidden?
- How could this scar become wisdom for someone else?
- Who in my life needs me to wield this weapon now?

The Flame Whispers
The enemy fears your scars.
Because every healed wound
is a weapon in your hand,
proof that nothing he tried
was wasted.

Chapter Nine
WALKING UNASHAMED

The Weight That Fell Away

For most of my life, fear was the invisible weight on my shoulders.
It bent my neck, shaped my voice, and dictated my silence.

Shame told me:

- "Don't speak—you'll sound foolish."
- "Don't show weakness—it'll be used against you."
- "Don't hope—you'll only be disappointed again."

But fear is a liar.
And the forge burned the lie away.

Now I walk in fear of One.
Not because I never stumble.
Not because I never feel the sting of failure.
But because fear no longer defines me.

Naked and Unafraid

Adam hid in the garden, clothed in fig leaves, because shame had entered the story.
Men have been hiding ever since—behind fig leaves, behind paychecks, behind silence.

Walking unashamed doesn't mean I'm without scars.
It means I no longer stitch fig leaves together to cover them.

I stand in the open.
Naked of masks.
Unashamed of the scars fire carved into my flesh and soul.

The Freedom of No Mask

There's a strange power in being unashamed.

It makes you fearless in places where men usually cower.
It gives you a voice where silence once reigned.
It frees you to laugh again, even in the face of storms.

Masks crack under pressure.
But a bare face can endure.
Because truth doesn't need disguise.

⚒ The Scroll Echo

Ground | Pulse | Swing

> **Ground:** The man bound by fear and silence.
> **Pulse:** The mask stripped away, scars revealed as proof.
> **Swing:** A man walking in the open—unashamed, fearless, free.

Unashamed Doesn't Mean Unchecked

Walking unashamed doesn't mean reckless bravado.
It doesn't mean flaunting scars for attention or using freedom to wound.
It means living with integrity so deep that no exposure can destroy you.
What's in the open can't be blackmailed.
What's confessed can't be weaponized.

Unashamed men are dangerous because they can't be bought,
can't be silenced,
can't be shamed back into chains.

The Witness of Freedom

Other men notice when you walk unashamed.
Some mock.
Some recoil.
But some—some lean in, because they've been waiting for proof that such a life is possible.

Your unashamed walk becomes a lantern for their path.
Not to show them your perfection,
but to prove that freedom is real.

A Word for the Reader

Brother, what fig leaves have you been hiding behind?
What lies has shame whispered in your ear?

Tear them away.
Walk out into the light.
Not flawless—
but fearless.

The world has enough masked men.
What it needs are reforged men, walking unashamed.

⚔ SIDEBAR: The Strength of the Unashamed

"What is revealed can no longer control you."

Answer and forge ahead:

- Where am I still hiding my scars?
- What conversations am I avoiding out of shame?
- Who could be set free if I walked openly, without fear?
- Where will I walk unmasked this week, so another man sees freedom is possible?

> ***The Flame Whispers***
> *You are not hidden.*
> *You are not bound.*
> *Step into the light—*
> *for what is revealed*
> *can never rule you again.*

Chapter Ten
THE CALL TO OTHER MEN

The Trumpet Sound

A reforged man cannot stay silent.
The fire was never just for me.
The scars were never just for me.
The silence broken in me is meant to break silence in others.

This is the call:
To sons who doubt their worth.
To brothers who hide in rivalry.
To fathers who fear they've failed.
To men everywhere still chained by shame and silence.

From Witness to Warrior

My story isn't a monument—it's a message.

If you can hear it, it means you're already being summoned.
Because the same fire that refined me is waiting for you.
The same Voice that whispered "You are not broken" is whispering now:
"You are not too far gone. You are not beyond the forge."

This call is not polite—it's a war trumpet.
And once you hear it, you cannot unhear it.

What Men Must Lay Down

The call is simple, but it will cost you everything:

- Lay down the mask of perfection.
- Lay down the silence of shame.

- Lay down the weapons you've used to wound instead of protect.
- Lay down the belief that you are too far gone.

Only then can the fire forge you into what you were meant to be.

⚒ The Scroll Echo

Ground | Pulse | Swing

> **Ground:** The man reforged.
> **Pulse:** His voice becomes a witness.
> **Swing:** That witness becomes a trumpet, calling others into the forge.

The Brotherhood Awakens

Something happens when one man answers the call.
Others start to rise.

- One scarred man opens up, and another finds courage to confess.
- One weary father admits his failures, and another discovers he's not alone.
- One man throws off shame, and others start tearing off their fig leaves.

The call is contagious.
Brotherhood begins not with strength, but with honesty.
And honesty, when forged in fire, is stronger than iron.

The Enemy Fears the Call

The enemy doesn't tremble at isolated men.
He trembles at men rising together.

Because when one man reforged becomes ten,
and ten become a hundred,
and a hundred become a generation,
the silence is shattered forever.

What was once a scattered band of wounded men
becomes an army of warriors,
each carrying scars sharpened into weapons.

A Word for the Reader

Brother—this is your moment.
Not tomorrow. Not after you clean yourself up.
Now.

The trumpet is sounding.
The fire is ready.
The forge is waiting.

Do not hide.
Do not delay.
Answer the call.

SIDEBAR: The Trumpet Test

> **"When the call comes, a man has two choices: hide in shame, or rise in fire."**

Answer and forge ahead:

- Who in my life is waiting to see me rise?
- Who will I call or text today with honesty instead of silence?
- Will I live as one reforged—or remain silent in the shadows?
- What keeps me from answering the call today?

The Flame Whispers
Do not wait.
Do not hide.
The trumpet is sounding,
and the forge is open.
Rise—now.

Chapter Eleven
THE BROTHERHOOD RESTORED

From Isolation to Brotherhood

For too long, men have fought alone.
Each carrying wounds in silence.
Each pretending strength while bleeding inside.

Isolation is the oldest trap.
It makes every man believe his struggle is unique, his shame unbearable, his voice unworthy.

But when reforged men come together, the lie breaks.
We discover that what nearly killed us in secret becomes the very ground of our shared strength.

The Forge Was Never Meant to Be Lonely

The fire is personal, yes—but it's never private.
The blacksmith doesn't forge one blade and stop.
He forges an armory.

That's what brotherhood is:
a line of sharpened men,
standing shoulder to shoulder,
not competing, not hiding,
but restoring each other's heart and soul.

⚒ The Scroll Echo

Ground | Pulse | Swing

> **Ground:** Men once scattered, isolated, divided.
> **Pulse:** Reforged individually in fire.

Swing: Rising together as brothers, united in strength and purpose.

Brothers, Not Rivals

The world has trained us to see each other as competitors.
Whose paycheck is bigger.
Whose muscles are stronger.
Whose family looks cleaner on the outside.

But in the forge, comparison dies.
No blade asks another how sharp it is.
It only asks: "Will you stand with me when the strike comes?"

Brotherhood restores what rivalry destroyed.

The Armor of Brotherhood

A single man reforged is dangerous.
But a brotherhood reforged is unstoppable.

- When one falters, the others lift him.
- When one is attacked, the others surround him.
- When one forgets his worth, the others remind him who he is.

This is not weakness.
This is the greatest strength men will ever know.
Not independence—interdependence.
Not to cover up each other's faults, but to restore what was lost and share the win.

The Restoration of Trust

Trust doesn't come easy.
It is born through scars shown and not mocked.

Through confessions given and not weaponized.
Through failures shared and not exploited.

Brotherhood is restored one honest word at a time,
one scar revealed at a time,
one man choosing to protect instead of prey on another.

This is what heals the fracture in men's souls.

A Word for the Reader

Brother, who is standing with you?
Who have you allowed into your fire?

If the answer is no one,
then hear this truth: you were not meant to walk alone.

Find brothers.
Stand together.
Restore the bond the world tried to break.

⚒ SIDEBAR: Signs of True Brotherhood

> **"Brotherhood is not found in the noise of the crowd, but in the silence of trust."**

Answer and forge ahead:

- Who in my life do I trust with my scars?
- Have I mistaken rivalry for brotherhood?
- How can I begin restoring trust with the men around me?
- What step will I take to build or repair trust with one brother this week?

The Flame Whispers
You were never meant to stand alone.
The forge has made you a brother—
and your strength is not only your own.
Rise together and the armory is complete.

Chapter Twelve
FATHERS OF FIRE

The Wound of the Absent Father

Every man carries his father's shadow.
For some, it was a presence so heavy it crushed.
For others, it was an absence so vast it hollowed.

The silence of fathers breeds silence in sons.
The anger of fathers breeds anger in sons.
The neglect of fathers breeds neglect in sons.

But the forge breaks the cycle.
A man reforged does not hand down silence—he hands down fire.

The Fire Passed Down

True fatherhood is not about perfect advice or spotless history.
It's about carrying fire in your hands and passing it on.

Fire that warms, not burns.
Fire that refines, not consumes.
Fire that guides, not blinds.

When a reforged man steps into fatherhood,
he becomes a hearth for his children—
a place where they are shaped by truth, not lies;
strengthened by love, not fear.

⚒ The Scroll Echo

Ground | Pulse | Swing

> **Ground:** Sons broken under silence, anger, or absence.

Pulse: Men reforged in the fire of their own trials.
Swing: Fathers of fire—breaking the cycle, raising children in courage and love.

Fatherhood Beyond Blood

Not every man will have biological children.
But every reforged man will father someone.

A nephew.
A neighbor.
A young man at work who has no one to guide him.

Fatherhood is not limited to lineage.
It is the mantle of any man who carries wisdom, love, and fire.

Healing the Father Wound

Many men hesitate to step into fatherhood because they still carry the wound of their own fathers.

Here is the truth:

- You are not bound to repeat their silence.
- You are not destined to mirror their failures.
- You are not trapped by what you did not receive.

The fire can heal what was withheld.
The forge can turn your father's absence into your children's abundance.

What Fathers of Fire Give

1. **Presence** – showing up, not disappearing.
2. **Voice** – speaking blessing, not withholding it.
3. **Boundaries** – protecting without controlling.
4. **Example** – living the truth, not just preaching it.
5. **Legacy** – leaving fire, not ashes.

The Generational Swing

Fathers of fire are not just raising children—they are raising generations.

When one man reforged becomes one father of fire,
his flame lights the torches of sons and daughters
who will carry it farther than he ever could.

This is how legacies shift.
This is how nations turn.
This is how silence dies.

A Word for the Reader

Brother, what kind of father will you be?
Not just to your children,
but in the world around you?

The forge has prepared you for this mantle.
Step into it.
Raise sons of flame and daughters of fire.

❈ SIDEBAR: The Father's Blessing

> **"Every child is waiting for one word: you are enough—and one gift: a fire to carry forward."**

Answer and forge ahead:

- What wound did my father leave in me?
- How can I break that cycle and become a source of guidance?
- Who around me needs my fire, even if they don't carry my blood?
- What word of blessing will I speak today to someone I lead or love?

The Flame Whispers
You are not bound to your father's silence.
You are not chained to his shadow.
The fire has come to you—
carry it forward,
and raise sons and daughters of flame.

Chapter Thirteen
SONS OF FLAME

The Spark Carried Forward

Every reforged man carries a choice:
Will the fire end with me,
or will it ignite in those who follow?

Sons of flame are not born by accident.
They are kindled.
They are sparked by the presence, voice, and courage of fathers of fire.

Breaking the Inheritance of Ash

Too many men have inherited only ash:

- Ashes of broken promises.
- Ashes of abandoned homes.
- Ashes of anger without explanation.

But a reforged man passes on flame, not ash.
He hands his children something alive—
something that will burn long after he is gone.

⚒ The Scroll Echo

Ground | Pulse | Swing

> **Ground:** Sons inherit silence or scars without guidance.
> **Pulse:** Fathers of fire pass down flame instead of ash.
> **Swing:** Sons of flame rise, carrying the torch farther than their fathers.

Sons Who Burn Bright

A son of flame grows up knowing:

- **He is seen.** His father's eyes are on him—not only when he fails but when he rises.
- **He is spoken over.** His father's words are life, not silence.
- **He is strengthened.** His father teaches him how to stand in fire without fear.

This kind of son burns brighter, not because he avoids the fire, but because he knows how to walk through it without being consumed.

Daughters of Flame

And let it be said—daughters are not left in the cold.
They too inherit the fire.

A daughter of flame grows secure in her worth,
unashamed of her voice,
unafraid of her strength.

When a father of fire raises daughters,
he teaches them they are not fragile candles—
they are torches meant to light the dark.

The Generational Swing

The beauty of flame is this:
It multiplies.
One torch lights another without losing itself.

So it is with men reforged.
Your fire becomes your son's fire.
Your courage becomes your daughter's courage.

Your faith becomes the foundation for a future you may never see.

This is how silence dies across generations.
This is how shame loses its grip.
This is how the reforging of one man becomes the restoration of a lineage.

A Word for the Reader

Brother, Answer, and forge ahead:

- What will my sons inherit from me—flame or ash?
- What will my daughters carry into the world—fear or fire?
- Will my legacy end with survival, or begin with flame?

    The Choice is already burning in my hands.

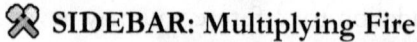 **SIDEBAR: Multiplying Fire**

> **"A single torch can light a thousand others without dimming its flame."**

Answer and forge ahead:

- Where have I seen the flame of courage pass from one man to another?
- Who in my life is waiting for me to hand them fire?
- How can I live so my legacy burns bright in generations yet unborn?
- What torch will I hand to my son, daughter, or another today?

The Flame Whispers
The fire was never meant to end with you.
Pass it on.
Light the next torch.
And watch the dark retreat
before a thousand sons and daughters of flame.

Chapter Fourteen
THE REFORGED LEGACY

The Echo Beyond the Forge

The work of reforging is never just about one man.
It begins in the fire of personal trial,
but the echo reaches farther—
to sons and daughters,
to brothers and friends,
to a community starving for truth.

The reforged legacy is this:
a life that keeps burning long after the man is gone.

From Wound to Witness

The wound that once silenced you
becomes the witness that awakens others.

Your scars are no longer marks of shame—
they are maps for the next generation.
Proof that the fire does not destroy,
it transforms.

Every man who rises from silence
writes a new story into the bloodline.

⚒ The Scroll Echo

Ground | Pulse | Swing

> **Ground:** Generations marked by silence, shame, and broken cycles.
> **Pulse:** One man reforged in the fire of trial.

Swing: Entire lineages restored, communities strengthened, legacies redefined.

The Ripple of One Life

History remembers warriors and kings,
but heaven records fathers who broke cycles.

One man who chooses to live as a son restored
becomes a father of fire.
That father raises sons and daughters of flame.
And those children carry the torch into a world
that never knew how dark it was until light began to spread.

Your reforging is not small—it is cosmic, generational, eternal.

Legacy is Not Wealth, But Fire

The world says legacy is money left behind,
names carved in stone,
buildings bearing your name.

But a reforged man knows better:
Legacy is not what you leave in your bank account—
it is what you leave in your bloodline.

Legacy is not your reputation—
it is your *resonance*.

The resonance of truth.
The resonance of courage.
The resonance of fire that does not die.

Communities Reborn

When enough men rise,
villages change.
Workplaces shift.
Even nations tremble.

Why?
Because silence loses its grip when men speak truth.
Because violence breaks when men choose mercy.
Because shame crumbles when men walk unashamed.

Communities don't need more slogans.
They need men reforged—
men who carry legacies of fire into every street, every home, every heart.

The Generational Swing

Imagine a man reforged.
He fathers in fire.
His sons and daughters rise as flame.
Their children are torches in a darker world.

Within three generations,
what was once a line of silence and shame
becomes a lineage of fire and freedom.

That is the reforged legacy.
Not a monument of stone,
but a wildfire of truth.

A Word for the Reader

Brother, your legacy is being forged now.
Not tomorrow.
Not someday.

Every scar you reveal,
every truth you speak,
every son or daughter you ignite—
this is the mark you leave on the world.

Answer and forge ahead:

- Am I passing down fire or ash?
- Am I leaving silence or song?
- Will my children remember my absence—or my flame?

⚔ SIDEBAR: The Weight of Legacy

> **"Legacy is not measured by how long your name is remembered, but by how deeply your fire burns in others."**

Answer and forge ahead:

- Who taught me what legacy meant—and do I agree with them?
- How can I reframe my past so my scars become torches, not chains?
- What scar will I reveal as testimony so my legacy burns brighter?
- What will the generations after me inherit because I chose to be reforged?

The Flame Whispers
Your scars are not just yours.
Your fire is not just yours.
Pass them on,
and your legacy will burn
long after your name is gone.

Chapter Fifteen
THE WEAPON OF WISDOM

The Forge of Pain

Every wound tells a story.
Every scar hides a lesson.

For years, pain feels like theft—
a robber that steals youth, peace, and joy.
But in the forge, pain becomes teacher.
And what once was a mark of shame
is reforged into a weapon of wisdom.

Wisdom From the Wound

Men who walk unbroken lives may shine briefly,
but they lack the steel of scars.

A reforged man knows:

- **What betrayal feels like—**so he becomes trustworthy.
- **What silence does to the soul—**so he becomes a voice.
- **What abandonment leaves behind—**so he chooses presence, even when it costs.

The wound does not define him.
But it arms him.

⚒ The Scroll Echo

Ground | Pulse | Swing

> **Ground:** Pain received as punishment, leaving men bitter or broken.

Pulse: Pain embraced as instruction, scars understood as teachers.
Swing: Wisdom weaponized—scars turned into blades that cut lies, heal wounds, and free others.

Turning Scars Into Swords

The enemy thought your pain would silence you.
Instead, it gave you language.
The shame meant to cripple you
became the strength that steadied you.

Your scar is your sword.
Your failure is your teaching.

This is why reforged men cannot be controlled by the past.
They have turned it into a weapon.

Wisdom Cuts Differently

The world swings swords of anger, vengeance, and pride.
But the reforged man swings wisdom.

His strike is sharper than rage.
His patience is stronger than force.
His presence disarms more than violence ever could.

Wisdom is not soft—it is fire tempered with truth.
It is strength that endures long after raw power burns out.

Brothers Armed Together

When a band of reforged men gather,
their scars form an armory.

One brings the wisdom of survival.
Another brings the wisdom of forgiveness.
Another brings the wisdom of endurance.
Together, they form an armory no enemy can withstand.

This is why community matters.
No one man carries every weapon.
But together, reforged men are unstoppable.

The Generational Swing

When fathers of fire pass down wisdom,
sons of flame don't repeat their mistakes.
They learn without having to bleed in the same places.

Wisdom is the inheritance that multiplies fire without repeating ash.
It saves time.
It redeems pain.
It writes a new future.

A Word for the Reader

Brother, look at your scars.

- Which ones still ache?
- Which ones have taught you something unshakable?
- Which ones are you ready to turn into weapons for others?

Your wisdom is not wasted.
Your pain is not pointless.
Your fire is not finished.

⚔ SIDEBAR: Scarred but Armed

> "Every scar is proof of survival. Every survival is a weapon of wisdom."

Questions for freedom:

- What lesson has pain taught me that no book could?
- Who needs to hear the wisdom I carry, even if it came at a cost?
- How can I swing my scars like a sword to cut lies and free others?
- Who could be freed today if I shared one scar as wisdom?

The Flame Whispers
Your scars are not shame.
They are swords.
Swing them with wisdom—
for the lies you cut today
become the freedom of tomorrow

Chapter Sixteen
THE QUIET GENERAL

Reforged men lead, not by shouting, but by scars and steady fire.

The Myth of the Loud Commander

The world mistakes volume for authority.
It thinks leadership is barked orders and clenched fists.
But real command is quieter than that.

A true general doesn't need to prove he's in charge.
His scars do the talking.
His presence settles the room.
His fire warms his men before it ever warns his enemies.

You don't follow him because you fear him.
You follow him because you trust where he's going.

Why the General is Quiet

He has nothing to hide.
He's already stood at the breaking point and didn't run.
He's already learned that rage can win a moment and lose a man.

So he leads with **strength under control—**
power that could crush, but chooses to carry.

Quiet isn't weakness—it's confidence scarred and refined in the forge.

The Three Laws of the Quiet General

1. **Presence before Plan**
   Show up first. Breathe. See. Listen. Then move.

(A bad plan with a steady presence beats a perfect plan shouted from a distance.)

2. **Principle over Pressure**
   Pressure screams for shortcuts.
   Principle whispers, Take the next right step.
   The Quiet General chooses the whisper.

3. **People before Problem**
   Fix the man and the man can fix the machine.
   Break the man and even a fixed machine will fail.

Command Voice vs. Father Voice

He has two voices, both tempered by fire:

- **Command Voice:** Clear, sparse, unafraid of silence between words.
  Used for danger, deadlines, and decisive moments. No theatrics—just direction.

- **Father Voice:** Warm, honest, steady.
  Used for correction, blessing, restoration. Doesn't humiliate; restores dignity.

He knows when to switch. That's wisdom, not performance.

The Weight He Carries (and How He Carries It)

- **Responsibility without Rescue:** He owns outcomes, but doesn't steal growth from his people by solving everything for them.
- **Boundaries without Bitterness:** He says no without apology and yes without resentment.

- **Truth without Theater:** No posturing, no show—just reality stated with courage.

He has learned the difference between control and care: control cages; care cultivates.

Field Manual: Tactics of the Quiet General

- **Stand** — Take ground with your feet first, not your mouth.
- **See** — Observe the field; do not lead blind.
- **Name** — Call the truth by its real name (fear, pride, fatigue, confusion).
- **Assign** — Place strengths where they matter; don't punish weakness—pair it.
- **Shield** — Take public blame, give public credit. (Your men will cross fire for you.)
- **AAR Ritual** — Run After-Action Reviews without shame:
    - What happened?
    - What helped?
    - What hurt?
    - What's the one change we make next time? No speeches. No excuses. Just growth.
- **Bless & Correct** — Correction in private; blessing in public.
- **Rotate the Torch** — Let others lead small missions. Fire multiplies when shared.

Where He Leads (Home, Work, Battle)

Home: He shows up to boring Tuesdays.
He blesses out loud. He apologizes fast.
He keeps promises small and keeps them anyway.

Work: He builds apprentices, not dependents.
He teaches how to think, not just what to do.
He leaves systems that outlast him.

Battle: He is first to arrive and last to leave.
He sees the quiet man in the back and asks him the question no one thought to.

The Cost He Accepts

Leadership will misread you.
Some will call your quiet "weak."
Some will beg you to be louder, harsher, faster.

But the Quiet General remembers:

- Panic is contagious.
- So is peace.
  He chooses which one to spread.

He also accepts this cost:
You will not be thanked right away.
You're building men, not applause.

When to be Loud

Silence is a tool, not a religion.
There are moments to thunder:

- When wolves are in the fold.
- When truth is being twisted.
- When the weak are being used as shields.
- When delay equals damage.

Then his voice is a trumpet—brief, surgical, unmistakable.
He doesn't stay loud; he strikes and returns to steady.

⚒ The Scroll Echo

Ground | Pulse | Swing

> **Ground:** A man once led by rage, masks, and noise.
> **Pulse:** Reforged into presence, principle, and patient strength.
> **Swing:** He becomes a Quiet General—fathering, shielding, and guiding others through fire.

What Follows a Quiet General

- **Order without oppression.**
- **Courage without bravado.**
- **Loyalty without fear.**
- **Results without wreckage.**

Men under him stop pretending.
They start telling the truth faster.
They volunteer for hard things.
They take care of each other when he's not in the room.
That's command you can't counterfeit.

A Note on Failure

He still fails.
When he does, he owns it fully and quickly:

"I missed it."
"I spoke from fear."
"I pushed pace over people."
"I'm going to repair this; here's how."

His men don't need a flawless commander.
They need a **truthful** one.

A Word for the Reader

Brother, where is your leadership loud but empty?
Where is it quiet but absent?

Answer and forge ahead:

- **Presence:** Do I show up first—or manage from a distance?
- **People:** Who on my team/family needs my Father Voice today?
- **Principle:** Where am I letting pressure replace what I know is right?
- **Process:** What's the one AAR question I'm avoiding?

You don't need a new personality.
You need a steadier fire.

⚔ SIDEBAR: Rules of Engagement

> **"Lead with presence. Correct with honor. Decide with principle. Leave people stronger than you found them."**

Quick checks:

- If I vanished today, did I build someone who can carry the torch?
- Did my words add oxygen to the fire—or smoke to the room?
- Am I protecting the mission and the men?
- What moment today needs my presence more than my words?

> ***The Flame Whispers***
> *Command without theater.*
> *Shield without fear.*
> *Do not mistake silence for surrender—*
> *the quiet fire is the fiercest flame.*
> *Be still when wisdom leads,*
> *be loud when wolves appear,*
> *and let your scars settle the field.*
> *The Quiet General needs no applause—*
> *his fire is already followed.*

Chapter Seventeen
THE FORGE OF BROTHERHOOD

Men reforged alone are strong; men reforged together are unbreakable.

The Lie of the Lone Wolf

The lone wolf is a myth.
It's a story told by broken men to hide how hungry they are.
The world glorifies the self-made man—silent, unshaken, untouchable.
But here's the truth: lone wolves starve.

Wolves survive in packs. Armies win in ranks.
Steel is strongest when forged beside other steel.
A blade forged alone may look sharp,
but it will crack at the first real blow.

The fire that reforged you wasn't meant to end with you.
You were tempered for the man next to you.

Brotherhood Is Born in Fire, Not in Comfort

Brotherhood doesn't grow in ease.
It's born in trenches where mud and blood mix.
It's found in night shifts where fatigue rips off the mask.
It's revealed in confessions—where silence breaks and truth spills raw.

Comfort breeds acquaintances.
Battle births brothers.

A Testimony of Fire

I learned early what happens when brotherhood collapses.

My mother's brother once threatened her with a knife—over twenty dollars.
And she brought me, a small boy, to stand between her and danger.
What kind of world asks a child to guard a mother from her own blood?
I numbed it out, because boys have no language for betrayal that close.
But it stayed—the silence afterward, the proof that when men betray their own, something holy is lost.

Years later, I stood beside the 34.5kV lines.
That hum of the transformer isn't a clean note—it's a broken banjo in low E, buzzing in the air with danger: *Make a mistake and you're done.*
In that sound I learned what real brotherhood meant.
My crew didn't need bravado—they needed presence.
A calm word. A steady spirit. A man who wouldn't flinch when the hum pressed fear into their chest.
That's where brotherhood is born: in the fire that can kill you, where one man's steadiness keeps another alive.

Isolation lies—it tells you to carry pain alone.
But scars carried in silence only rot. Scars revealed become warnings for brothers.

And then came my son.
My heartache. My hope.
Poor choices carved paths he had to walk, mistakes he had to pay for.
I wanted to carry his weight. But brotherhood is not always rescue.
Sometimes it is the painful love that refuses to quit,
the voice that says: This is not the end. You are not broken.
Even when fire burns both of you.

Marks of a Reforged Brotherhood

- **Shared Scars** — We don't compare wounds; we show them. Your scar says: I bled here, and I lived. You can too.
- **Mutual Burden** — A true brother doesn't just pat your back; he helps carry your pack. Sometimes he carries you.
- **Honest Steel** — Sparks fly when iron sharpens iron. Brotherhood isn't flattery—it's friction that proves strength.

Field Manual: Building the Forge

- **Presence** — Show up consistently. Brotherhood dies in absence.
- **Transparency** — No masks; scars speak louder than stories.
- **Trust** — Keep confidences. What's shared in the forge stays there.
- **Trial** — Do something hard together: climb, fight, build, pray, fast.
- **Table** — Eat together; bread breaks barriers.
- **Testimony** — Tell the truth, even when it costs. Lies rot the forge from within.
-

The Enemy of Brotherhood

Isolation whispers: *You're fine alone.*
Shame hisses: *If they knew, they'd walk away.*
Pride sneers: *You don't need them—you're stronger by yourself.*

These are the same voices that leave men broken in silence.
The forge rejects them.
The forge answers back: *We rise or fall together. You're not carried because you're weak—you're carried because you're ours.*

Why Brotherhood Matters

Strength multiplies: one torch can light a room, ten can light a city.
Blind spots close: alone, you miss angles; together, you cover flanks.
Courage endures: a lone man may falter; a brother's voice at his back steadies the line.

Leadership without brotherhood becomes tyranny.
Brotherhood without leadership becomes chaos.
Together they form the shield wall that does not break.

⚒ The Scroll Echo

Ground | Pulse | Swing

> **Ground:** Scarred, convinced I could survive alone.
> **Pulse:** Another scarred man saying: "Me too."
> **Swing:** The forge burned hotter; we rose shoulder to shoulder, unbreakable.

A Word for the Reader

If you've been walking like a lone wolf—
shoulders heavy, scars hidden, convincing yourself you're fine—
hear me: you're not meant to carry it all.

Brotherhood isn't weakness.
It's the furnace where strength is tempered and scars are given meaning.

The burden you hide will only crush you.
The scar you bury will only fester.
But when you reveal them in the forge, they become the steel that sharpens another man's blade.

Brother, you are not broken.
You are being reforged.
And the brotherhood is proof that you were always meant to stand, not alone, but side by side.

⚒ SIDEBAR: Brotherhood

> "Alone, the fire only burns.
> Together, the fire forges."

Answer and forge ahead:

- Where am I still living as a lone wolf, starving inside?
- Who has God already placed beside me that I have not trusted yet?
- What burden am I hiding that was never meant to be shouldered alone?
- Who will I invite into my fire this week instead of walking alone?

The Flame Whispers
One blade alone will crack.
Drop the mask,
and share the scar.
Brotherhood is fire shared—
and fire shared does not die.

Chapter Eighteen
THE SILENT MARCH

Strength proven in quiet endurance—brotherhood walking in the dark, unbroken.

The Silent March Is the Real Forge

Brotherhood is not proven in the roar of battle.
It is proven in the quiet march between the battles—
the long stretch when no one is cheering,
when old scars ache in the quiet,
when the world seems to have moved on.

The silent march is the real forge.
It's the slow walk home after the fire.
It's the mornings before the tools are lifted.
It's the nights when the voices of regret try to whisper louder than the Spirit.

As a boy, silence was the blanket thrown over betrayal.
It was numbness—a way to survive what I could not name.
But as a man, silence became a test.
Would I let unspoken pain eat me alive,
or would I let silence become the place where I listen for the Voice that never lies?

The Brotherhood of Silence

In brotherhood, silence is not absence. It is agreement.

It's the knowing glance on the line,
the unspoken prayer when a brother breaks down,
the strength of a man walking beside you,
saying nothing, because nothing needs to be said.

Men reforged do not always roar.
Sometimes we move with the steady rhythm of silence—
a discipline learned through scars, a gravity the world cannot ignore.

What Silence Gives

- **Endurance without applause.**
- **Strength without boasting.**
- **Presence that outlasts words.**

When men walk together in silence, the world notices.
There is a weight to a man who has walked through fire
and chosen not to break then brag.
His silence is louder than speeches:
We are still here. We are not broken. We will not abandon one another.

Brotherhood is tested in the fire,
but it is proven in the silent march.

⚒ The Scroll Echo

Ground | Pulse | Swing

> **Ground:** Silence once buried me.
> **Pulse:** The whisper broke through.
> **Swing:** Now, silence carries strength instead of shame.

A Word for the Reader

- What silence in your life is still a wound?
- What silence could become strength if you let it?
- Who can I walk beside in quiet strength this week, without needing to fix them?
- Who will you choose to walk beside you, even when words fail?

⚒ SIDEBAR: The Silent March

> "Brotherhood is tested in fire.
> It is proven in silence."

Midpoint Recap

The Hammer Falls. The Steel Holds. The man rises.

You've seen the fire.
You've felt the silence.
You've carried the armor, worn the masks, and watched them shatter.
You've heard the whisper that said, You are not broken.
You've stepped into the forge—hammer, anvil, fire—and begun to rise as son, brother, father.

From there the flame spread:

- Wounds turned into weapons.
- Scars became swords.
- Masks fell, shame broke, and men began to walk unashamed.

Then the call went out.
The trumpet summoned brothers.
The lone wolves came in from the cold.
And a brotherhood rose—scars revealed, burdens shared, iron sharpening iron.

Finally, silence itself was redeemed.
No longer a tomb, but a march.
No longer a wound, but a witness.

The silent march of reforged men—steady, scarred, unbroken.

> This is the turning point.
> The fire has proven you.
> The silence has tempered you.
> Brotherhood has bound you.

The question now is not whether you will rise.
It is how far the fire will spread.

> ***The Flame Whispers***
> *The march is long.*
> *The silence is heavy.*
> *The silent march is the forge no fire can imitate.*
> *Here men prove endurance,*
> *Hold the line.*
> *Walk unbroken, shoulder to shoulder.*
> *The fire spread this far—*
> *and the march will carry it farther.*

Chapter Nineteen
THE FINAL ASCENT

The last climb—calling every lesson, every scar, into the open.

The Summit Ahead

There comes a point in every journey where the air gets thin.
The easy ground is behind you.
The fire has done its work; the scars have hardened.
What's left is the climb.

This is the final ascent—
the summit most men never reach,
because it demands everything you've learned,
every scar you carry,
every lesson of brotherhood, silence, and flame.

You will be tempted to settle.
To camp in comfort,
to rest on what you've already survived,
to fall back into believing survival was the goal.
But the forge never calls a man to complacency.
It calls you higher.

What the Final Ascent Requires

- **Relentless Honesty** — You can't lie to yourself at altitude.
  The mask won't fit in thin air.
  The truth finds you and demands a verdict:
  Will you live as the man you have become,
  or will you shrink back into the man you were?

- **Brotherhood at Your Side** — The summit is not for solo climbers.

This is where you lean on men you trust—
the ones who've seen your scars,
the ones who've carried your burdens,
the ones who don't let you quit on the coldest morning.

- **Courage to Leave Old Ground —** The hardest step is always the next one.
  It's letting go of the safe pain, the familiar struggle,
  and daring to put your foot where there is only hope.

- **Vision for What Lies Beyond —** The final ascent is not about looking down at what you survived,
  but up—
  to the calling legacy—
  the fire meant to blaze for generations.

The Ground of the Overcomer

This is the ground of the overcomer.
It's the moment you stop asking,
"Am I broken?"
and start asking,
"Who will I become now that I am reforged?"

⚒ The Scroll Echo

Ground | Pulse | Swing

Ground: The wounds and scars that made you.
Pulse: The brotherhood and silence that carried you.
Swing: The climb—out of the valley, up the mountain, into the fullness of who you are.

A Word for the Reader

- Where have you settled for survival instead of climbing for freedom?
- What vision are you climbing toward that's bigger than your own story?
- Who are you climbing with—and who have you left behind?
- What step of courage can I take today that pulls me higher than survival?

⚔ SIDEBAR: The Final Ascent

"Every scar is a rung.
Every brother is a handhold.
Every step is a decision not to go back."

The Flame Whispers
Do not camp in comfort.
Do not bow to thin air.
Step higher.
Pull your brother with you.
The summit is not for the perfect—
it is for the reforged.

Chapter Twenty
THE VIEW FROM THE SUMMIT

The vantage point—seeing scars as strength, brotherhood as proof, and fire as witness.

The Summit Is Not the End

You reach the top and the wind is different.
It's not quieter—
it's clearer.
You can see where you've been.
But more than that, you can see where you are meant to go.

The summit is not the end of the journey.
It is the vantage point.
From here, you see the scars that once shamed you are now your armor.
The burdens you carried have become strength in your stride.
The brothers you trusted have become the proof that no man is meant to walk alone.

This is the place where you finally understand:
The pain was not the enemy—
the silence was not a tomb—
the fire was not a curse.
It was all preparation.

What the Summit Reveals

At the summit, a man sees three things clearly:

- **Where he came from.**
  The wounds, the failures, the betrayals—
  all the broken ground that tried to swallow him.
  He no longer fears those memories.

He honors them as the forge.

- **Who he stands with.**
  The men who helped him rise.
  The brothers who lent their strength,
  the sons and daughters waiting for his example.
  He sees that legacy is not built by one,
  but by many—standing linked, not scattered.

- **What comes next.**
  The summit is a call.
  Not to rest, but to witness.
  To carry the fire down the mountain,
  to light the way for those still climbing,
  to tell the truth that every scar bears light.

The Witness From the Summit

You are not broken.
You are a living witness.
From the summit, your voice echoes farther than your shadow ever reached.

⚒ The Scroll Echo

Ground | Pulse | Swing

> **Ground:** The trail behind—marked by scars, proof of survival.
> **Pulse:** The presence of brothers—every hand that steadied you, every voice that called you higher.
> **Swing:** The vision ahead—lighting the path for a thousand men to rise.

A Word for the Reader

- What would you say to the man at the bottom of the mountain?
- Who needs to hear one part of your story so they know the climb is possible?
- Who is waiting for your story to light their path?
- Will you stay on the summit—or descend to lead others up?

⚔ SIDEBAR: The Witness at the Summit

"A man's story is not for the echo chamber at the top.
It is the torch for the climb,
the signal fire for the lost,
the beacon for the brother who thinks he's alone."

The Flame Whispers
Do not stay at the top.
Do not keep the fire to yourself.
Descend with scars as light,
with brothers as shield,
and with your story as the beacon
for every man still climbing.

Final Chapter
THE COMMISSION: YOU ARE THE FIRE

The charge—rise, lead, witness. Your story is the torch.

The Blade Is Ready

There comes a moment when the forge goes silent.
Not because the work is over—
but because the blade is ready.

You, brother, are the blade.
You, brother, are the fire that did not die.

Every page you've read, every scar you've survived,
every night you doubted the light would come—
it all brings you to this:
You are not broken.
You are reforged.
You are the proof.

Now the world needs your witness.

Your Commission

This is your commission:

- **Carry your scars as credentials, not shame.**
- **Walk unashamed—so others see what freedom looks like.**
- **Stand with your brothers, even when words fail.**
- **Speak when silence is a prison for another man.**
- **Pass your fire on—teach, bless, correct, forgive.**
- **Leave no man behind—call every son, father, and brother to the forge.**

Your life is the echo.
Your story is the signal.
Your fire is the invitation.

Let no enemy, no regret, no old silence steal that from you.

⚒ The Scroll Echo — The Last Word

Ground | Pulse | Swing

> **Ground:** You survived.
> **Pulse:** You were never alone.
> **Swing:** Now you are the fire that calls others home.

Final Reflection

- Who will carry your fire when you're gone?
- What song will your scars sing?
- What will men say when your name is spoken— "He survived," or "He set me free"?
- Where will I carry the fire this week—home, work, or the street—so another man knows the forge is open?

⚒ SIDEBAR: The Living Proof

> "The world is not waiting for perfect men.
> The world is waiting for men who burn."

The Flame Whispers
Rise.
Burn.
Lead.
Heal.
Witness.
Brother, you are not broken—
you are the fire that will not die,
because His flame burns in you.

The Charge
Let this be your charge:
Go—burn, lead, heal, witness.
The world is darker without you.
The forge is open.
The fire is yours, waiting for you.

Brother, this book isn't just for your shelf.
It's a torch, a field manual, a resurrection song.
You are not broken.
You are the living proof that fire refines,
that scars can sing,
that brotherhood still saves.

Closing Meditation: The Blessing

Every scar tells a story, and every story is proof that brokenness isn't the end.

If you're still breathing, you're not beyond the fire.
Brother, neither am I.

This is your call: to rise, to be reforged, and to walk out of the furnace whole.
And as I speak it over you, I hear it whispered back to me.

You are not broken.
I am not broken.
We are the living proof that redemption is real.

Epilogue

And to the women who find themselves in these pages—know this: though these words were written to forge men, your scars and strength echo here too. You have carried the silence of fathers, the weight of brothers, the love of sons, and the fire of your own trials. This book honors you as well. For the reforging of a man is never his alone—the women beside him are part of the fire that shapes him.

Author's Note

Change begins with a choice. What you were is not what you must remain. Do not expect others to understand your change—show them. Prove it by the steadiness of your walk, the clarity of your voice, and the shift of your posture. Do not surrender to the lie that you are powerless. Think differently. Rise. Become the man you were forged to be. What is impossible with man is possible with God.

The Forge: Workbook Edition

This book was never meant to be read once and shelved. It was meant to be lived.

The Forge Workbook is your companion guide— filled with reflection prompts, scripture studies, and exercises that walk with you step by step through the fire.

Use it on your own. Use it with a brother. Use it with a group.

Wherever the forge finds you, this workbook is the anvil beneath your hammer.

Available on Amazon.com

The Quiet General — Action Page

The Three Laws

1. **Presence before Plan**
   - Show up first. Breathe. See. Listen. Then move.
   - A "good-enough plan + steady presence" beats a "perfect plan yelled from afar."

2. **People before Problem**
   - Fix the man and the man can fix the machine.
   - Protect dignity; coach skill.

3. **Principle over Pressure**
   - Pressure demands shortcuts; principle says: take the next right step.
   - If it costs integrity, it costs the mission later.

Command Voice vs. Father Voice
(When to Use Which)

- **Command Voice** → danger, deadlines, decisive moments
  - Short sentences. One action per line. No theatrics.
  - "Hold." "Shift left 10." "Kill power now."

- **Father Voice** → correction, blessing, restoration
  - Calm tone, human temperature. Private correction, public praise.
  - "Here's what I see. Here's how we fix it."
  - "How can we fix this together?"

Field Manual: Steps That Don't Miss

1. **Stand** — Put your feet on the ground before you put words in the air.

2. **See** — Walk the field. Ask two questions before one directive.

3. **Name** — Call the truth by its name (fatigue, fear, pride, confusion). Truth lowers the temperature.

4. **Assign** — Place strengths where they matter; pair weaknesses with cover.

5. **Shield** — Take public blame; give public credit. Loyalty compounds.

6. **AAR Ritual** — Normalize learning. (see template pg.127).

7. **Bless & Correct** — Correct in private; bless in public.

8. **Rotate the Torch** — Let others lead small missions; review, don't rescue.

After-Action Review (AAR)—12-Minute Template

Failure becomes wisdom only if captured. This is how you capture it.

When: ASAP while details are fresh (end of shift / end of day).
Who: Everyone involved (no spectators, no scapegoats).
Rules: No shame. No excuses. No monologues. Notes visible to all — no hidden minutes, no private edits.

1. **What happened?** (facts only; 2 minutes)
2. **What helped?** (keep doing)
3. **What hurt?** (stop/adjust)
4. **One change for next time?** (single, concrete tweak)
5. **Who owns it & by when?** (name + date)

Capture: 3 bullets max in a shared log (title, owner, due date). Follow-through: Start next shift by closing the loop on last AAR's actions.

Rules of Engagement (Pocket Checks)

- **Presence:** Did I actually show up where the friction is?
- **People:** Did my words protect dignity and build competence?
- **Principle:** Did I trade integrity for speed? (If yes, fix it now.)
- **Process:** Did we run an AAR and assign one change with an owner?

This book was never meant to stay on a shelf. Share it. Teach it. Pass the fire forward. If it reforged you, then carry the flame to another man who still believes he is broken.

"And we have known and believed the love that God hath to us. God is love; and he that dwelleth in love dwelleth in God, and God in him."
—1 John 4:16 (AKJV)

The forge is open. The fire is yours.

About the Author

Justin Butler Sr. knows the silence men carry and the scars they hide. Raised in chaos, forged in the fire of hard labor and leadership, and refined in the trials of fatherhood, he has walked the same ground he now calls other men to rise from.

As a trainer and mentor, Justin has spent years building men who work with steel, electricity, and fire—but his truest work is calling brothers to step out of silence and into brotherhood.

His life is proof that you are not broken.
You are being reforged.

Acknowledgments

To my wife: not always the most patient, but steadfast enough to withstand the forge. We walked through days neither of us enjoyed, yet by staying together we now share the fruit of endurance. Your truth has tempered me as much as fire — steady, shaping, undeniable.

To my old manager, Ryan, who once called me disrespectful, but then listened as I explained my upbringing and work environments. He responded with a sentence that changed my life: "It doesn't have to be that way." Those words reframed my entire past and gave me the courage to believe in something more.

To the one who simply showed up to instruct, to do their job. You may never know the power of the simple tactics and words you gave me.

To the few, trustworthy people who helped redirect my course when I only wanted to drift and "just be."

And since I was seventeen, to Yeshua. My strength, my Savior, and the fire that has never left me.

www.ingramcontent.com/pod-product-compliance
Lightning Source LLC
Chambersburg PA
CBHW071227090426
42736CB00014B/2999